# HAPPY CUSTOMERS FASTER CASH

USA chapters

A guide to effective communication in financial Customer Relationship Management

**Michael C. Dennis**

**Marcel Wiedenbrugge  -  Cliff Wynn**

Cover design: Patrick van der Doef

# Preface United States edition

During the more than two decades of my career, I have been privileged to have held a number of full-time positions in credit management in various industries. In this book, I have summarized many of the lessons I have learned during my career, particularly as it relates to the credit department's relationship with customers.

In credit management, we face multiple challenges including the need to collect accounts receivable quickly as well as the need to maintain customer goodwill. I am absolutely convinced that if your customers are happy about their interactions with the credit department, they are more likely to pay your invoices. This book, Happy Customers Faster Cash focuses on developing better working relationships with customers while, at the same time, maintaining customer goodwill.

While the views expressed in this book are the result of a significant amount of experience and effort, I respectfully ask readers to share their suggestions about how this book can be further improved.

Michael C. Dennis

San Francisco, California

# CONTENTS

CHAPTER 1: CREDIT MANAGEMENT IN THE UNITED STATES.................................5

1.1 Credit Management in the USA..........................................................6

1.2 Useful links about credit management, doing business and business culture in the USA..........................................................................................16

CHAPTER 2: COMMUNICATION WITH THE CUSTOMER........................................22

2.1 USA business culture and communication................................................23

BONUS CHAPTER

12 excuses for late payment and how to deal with them .......................................32

# CHAPTER 1: CREDIT MANAGEMENT IN THE UNITED STATES

## 1.1 Credit Management in the USA

During the last twenty-five years, credit management in the United States has changed significantly. Customers' buying power and buyers' knowledge and training has increased dramatically. This has fundamentally altered the bargaining power of companies offering open account credit terms --- placing customers more firmly in the 'driver's seat.'

There is an active credit management community in the U.S. Many credit professionals are willing to share information, knowledge and experience via various professional networks as well as in industry credit groups. Each of the NACM affiliates in the United States sponsors one or more industry credit groups. An industry credit group is made up of member creditor companies, each of whom sell into and extend credit to customers in a particular industry or business segment. Industry credit group meetings involve the exchange of factual historical information about their common customers including:

- Amount owing
- Amount past due
- How far past due

Gradually, credit management is moving toward a more integrated role in organizations. American companies increasingly understand that getting paid by debtor companies on-time is a vital part of doing successful business. American companies also recognize that there must be an appropriate relationship between the risk of non-payment (default or bad debt) and the financial reward associated with extending open account credit terms to customers and applicants.

More and more attention is paid to effective cross-functional communication, especially between the credit department and the sales team. Over time, credit team members have come to appreciate that the credit department's operations support the sales function, and that things go far more smoothly when there is a free flow of information between sales and credit enabling both departments to proactively address issues before they become problems, and resolve problems before they become critical.

American companies expect and require a close working relationship between sales and credit characterized by:

- A free and regular exchange of information between sales and credit.
- Timely responses from the credit team to inquiries from the sales department
- Consistency in the decisions made by the credit department, combined with a commitment to deliver 'bad news' to sales before the customer.
- Transparency and candor as it relates to the credit decision-making process, combined with the willingness to take as much time as necessary with sales to explain the rationale for your decision.
- A commitment not to 'blame' the salesperson when a credit decision that goes bad recognizing that the role of the salesperson is as an advocate for their customer.

- The ability to work proactively with sales to approve higher credit limits for customers before orders are submitted combined with the recognition that much more can be accomplished by working together than by working at cross purposes.
- Recognition that the role of the credit department is to monitor and manage the risk of non-payment and serious delinquency, not to eliminate all credit related risks.
- A willingness to listen, and to try to find creative solutions to credit related problems.
- A commitment to working with sales to help identify and to qualify new sales opportunities.
- A commitment to find a way to say *yes*, rather than to look for a reason to say *no* to open account terms and credit limits requested by sales on behalf of customers and applicants.

American companies' credit departments have become more reliant on the use of technology, including:

- Credit decision support software,
- Customer relationship management software and analytics,
- Deduction management software,
- Inbound and outbound communication platforms that enable online 24/7 availability,
- Collection management software,
- Enterprise resource planning software to manage the order hold and order approval process

Some companies give collectors unilateral authority to place accounts on credit hold, and then are surprised when customers and salespeople complain that credit holds are used too frequently, for the wrong reasons, or arbitrarily. Normally, a collector recommend a credit hold, but is not the person that approves a credit hold. Here are some general statements about the use of credit holds in the United States:

- Credit holds should be used infrequently, and only as a last resort.
- Often the threat of a credit hold is enough to persuade a reluctant customer to pay the outstanding debt.
- Sometimes, the debtor's accounts payable department will be told to hold payments until a creditor threatens to place the account on hold.
- Creditors usually try to give customers advanced notice of a credit hold.
- Many companies have at least one level of management sign-off before a credit hold is placed on an account.

### Perception of credit management

Over the past 10 years, credit management as a business function has become better understood. Awareness of the importance of credit management has risen since the start of the global credit crisis in 2008. However, when you ask an American business person who is not working in finance: "*Can you tell me what your credit management team is responsible for?*" they will often look puzzled and don't have an answer.

Automation of credit management is gradually becoming quite common, especially for larger and multinational companies. In the future, credit management will increasingly focus on integration with other business functions, data analysis and 24/7 availability (cloud solutions) and business process optimization.

**Credit policies**

Most American companies that sell on open account terms business to business (B2B) have some sort of formal credit policy. The length, scope and level of detail of these credit policies can vary significantly depending on the kind and complexity of a business. Some written policies include little more than a policy statement. Others include both policies and procedures. More comprehensive credit policies include a mission statement, policies, procedures, and detailed work instructions.

However, there are a number of companies who do business on open terms without having any specific credit policy in place. And there are many other companies with a policy that is out-of-date or irrelevant to daily operations. As a result, these policies are either entirely disregarded or at least partially ignored. Such creditor companies may also neglect to evaluate a new applicant carefully, or may have no process in place to regularly update credit files in order to check the creditworthiness of their existing customers. However, once confronted with one or more bad debt losses this cavalier or even negligent behavior usually changes quickly.

A company credit policy in the U.S. is likely to be not much different from a credit policy in other countries in the world. You can find many examples on various websites on how to set up a credit policy including these websites: www.encyclopediaofcredit.com.

**Credit Approval**

In some companies, the credit department needs to approve each sales order. It is more common for the credit department to be required to approve only those orders that exceed specific parameters. One example would be to approve all orders that would cause a customer to exceed the established credit limit. Ideally, there should be no way any order can bypass the credit approval process.

Parent – Subsidiary Relationships

In the U.S., a corporation can form another corporation. The company owning the other corporation is called the parent company. The company whose stock is owned by the other corporation is the subsidiary. A corporation that owns more than 50% percent of the common stock of another corporation is often referred to as the parent corporation.

**Payment terms**

Payment terms for credit sales vary from COD to Cash In Advance to 90 days and in rare cases even 120 days or more. The most common payment term in business to business in the U.S. is Net 30 days from date of invoice. When a company extends open account credit for 30 days, it usually does so without any guarantees that the debtor will issue payment. In this context, the term guarantee refers to credit enhancements such as a personal guaranty, an intercorporate guaranty, a letter of credit, a standby letter of credit, or a security interest in assets of the buyer/debtor.

## Payment delivery methods

Companies in the United States use a variety of methods for sending payments to their suppliers. One of the most common ways to remit payments to creditors is by electronic funds transfer (EFT). EFT is an inexpensive, reliable, fast and convenient mechanism for issuing and receiving payment. Another common payment mechanism is and remains payment by company check.  Direct debit is used occasionally in business-to-business transactions; however this usually involves a scenario in which the seller/supplier/creditor is in an unusually strong bargaining position relative to the customer/debtor company. The most popular electronic payment system for both consumers and small businesses is via a company credit card.   According to a report published by the Federal Reserve, for business to business bill payment in the U.S., the volume of electronic payments is rising rapidly.  Electronic payments include but are not limited to: ACH payments, Wire Transfers, Debit card payments and Credit card payments.  You can find more information about bill payment mechanisms at: www.frbservices.org/communications/payment_system_research.html

The U.S. banking market is dominated by four major banks: J.P. Morgan Chase and Company, Bank of America, Citigroup, and Wells Fargo and Company. Payments between accounts of the same bank are usually processed the same day. An electronic payment between two different U.S. banks usually takes about one day, as payments need to be processed through the Automated Clearinghouse. You can find more information about the Automated Clearinghouse at: www.nacha.org .

Wire Transfer on the other hand is a bank-to-bank transfer using the Federal Reserve System. Both the sending bank and receiving bank will charge fees for this service. However, the recipient will normally receive the money in the bank account the same day as it is sent by the remitting bank. You can find more information about the Federal Reserve System and wire transfers at: www.frbservices.org .

## Credit Information Providers and Credit Management Services

In this book, we focus on business-to-business credit decision-making only. The information infrastructure (online and offline) in the United States is quite advanced and well-organized. You can easily find or buy a wide variety of financial and commercial data on companies as well as consumers (private persons). For consumer related information, there are a large number of federal, state and in some cases local regulations governing the acquisition and dissemination of consumer credit information.

If the financial information presented to a creditor company by a customer or applicant is nothing but guesses or estimates, the financial data has little value, so whether or not financial statements are audited by a third-party CPA firm is an important consideration for the credit analyst. Third party credit bureaus make a point of stating whether or not a customer's financial statements reproduced in the credit report are audited or not. If you receive financial statements directly from a customer, whether or not the statements are audited by a CPA firm and the extent of that audit as well as the audit findings should be the first things to consider. To some extent, audits or lack of audited statements are a guide to the accuracy and the reliability of customer financial statements. You should carefully note the nature of the audit and the corresponding responsibility accepted by the accountant, both of which are expressed in the wording of Auditor's Opinion Letter sometimes referred to as the auditor's certification.

As used above, a CPA means a Certified Public Accountant. This is an individual who has satisfied the education and experience requirements, and has passed an examination required and necessary to be licensed as a CPA. A CPA firm is a company owned or at least staffed with CPAs licensed in the American state(s) in which the CPA firm operates. All CPAs are accountants. Not all accountants are CPAs.   The implication here is that when financial statements are not audited by a third party CPA firm, it is unclear how a credit professional would determine the accuracy of the information contained in those statements. It should also be noted that in the United States, the overwhelming majority of companies are privately held, and the overwhelming majority of privately held companies do not have and cannot provide creditors with audited financial statements.

Before analyzing customers' financial statements, you should review the auditor's opinion letter to determine the scope of the audit. Relative to financial statements and the use of outside auditors, there are basically four different types of opinion letters that can be submitted. They are:

- The Unqualified Opinion,
- A Qualified Opinion,
- An Adverse Opinion,
- A Disclaimer of Opinion.

### The Unqualified Opinion
An unqualified opinion letter involves a certification made by the independent CPA firm that the company's financial statements were prepared in conformity with Generally Accepted Accounting Principles [GAAP], and fairly represented the firm's financial condition on the statement date.

### A Qualified Opinion
A qualified auditor's opinion letter is one in which the CPA has included one or more specific qualifications to its assurance that the customer's financial statements follow GAAP. This means that one or more irregularities were found, and that the customer could not or would not correct these irregularities.

### An Adverse Opinion
Arguably the most serious of all the opinion letters that can accompany a customer's financial statements, when a CPA firm discovers information during the course of its audit that demonstrates material noncompliance with GAAP accounting rules, the CPA may choose to submit an adverse opinion letter to accompany the financial statements of the company under

review. An adverse opinion letter states that the customer's financial position is not fairly presented by the statements submitted. The auditor must provide specific reason(s) for an adverse opinion.

### A Disclaimer of Opinion

Based on any number of factors including but not limited to the scope of the audit conducted, a CPA may be unwilling to express any opinion about the accuracy of a customer's financial statements. The auditor is then said to have generated a disclaimer of opinion letter. This disclaimer means that the CPA form cannot and does not offer any assurance about the accuracy of the financial statements.

If you need information on U.S. based businesses, there are numerous service providers who can effectively help you to get reliable and [usually] up-to-date information. See chapter 1.3.1 for more information.

## Credit Insurance

Credit insurance minimizes the risk of non-payment due to financial, economic, or in some cases political uncertainties. Trade credit insurance can be a cost-effective mechanism for transferring credit risk. Insurance premiums are generally charged as a percentage of sales. Credit insurance premium rates are based on a number of factors including country risk, customer risk, the length of payment terms, and the trade creditor's loss experience. Credit insurance is a complicated product that should not be purchased without research to see what kind of policies are available, and what the differences are between and among the policies, and which policies seem to offer the best "fit" for your company and its needs. In the United States, credit insurance is not as widely used as it is in Western Europe. However, adoption rates are increasing rapidly.

## Consignment Sales

Under a consignment arrangement, the consignor delivers goods to the consignee. The consignor retains title to and ownership of the merchandise until the goods are sold by the consignee to a third party. When the goods are sold, the consignee becomes obligated to pay the consignor. The consignee receives a fee / commission for making the sale. If the consignee does not sell the goods, they may return them to the consignor without obligation. Consignments are not true sales because title does not pass to the consignee. One of the most obvious risks with consignment involves a scenario in which the goods are delivered to the consignee and sold but subsequently the consignor does not receive the payment it is owed.

## Export Credit Risk

In the United States, companies often consider exporting to be high risk. Despite this, credit departments are expected to find a way to sell without requiring the buyer to provide payment in advance or a Letter of Credit. A credit department needs to consider three factors in reviewing export sales. The first is the risk of payment default. The second is the risk of serious payment delinquency. The third is concern about actions taken by the government in the buyer's country that prevents the customer from issuing payment.

**Debt Collection**

In the United States, there are hundreds if not thousands of business-to-business commercial collection agencies. Due to fierce competition, collection agencies find the need to differentiate themselves. Some agencies focus on a particular niche, such as by specializing in specific business segments. Other agencies differentiate themselves by the manner in which they collect debts. For some, that means a telephone-only approach to collections. For other agencies, the approach used to written communication only. Others differentiate themselves by assigning collectors to visit delinquent debtors face-to-face to secure appropriate and specific payment commitments. There are no hard and fast rules about which approach works best.  What you need to know is what tools your collection agency uses so that you can be sure that the collection fees you pay are competitive based on the type of work the collection agency performs for you.  For example, you would expect the contingent collection rate to be higher at a collection agency that sends collectors to the debtor's place of business than the rate you would pay for a telephone only approach to debt collection.

Deciding which collection agency to use can be difficult. Many credit managers in the United States are inundated with calls from third party commercial collection agencies asking for their business. Some licensed collection agencies post bonds or carry errors and omissions insurance. A reputable collection agency could be a member of a member of one of several professional organizations such as the Commercial Law League of America's which publishes a list of Certified Commercial Collection Agencies at:  www.clla.org/sections/ccaa_list.cfm .

For more detailed information about rules and regulations for commercial debt collection in the U.S. please refer to chapter 1.3.1 on "debt collection".

In the United States, the typical collection agency services include:

- A free final demand service; sent from the collection agency to the debtor
- Access to the collection agency's database; to review the collection agency's experience collecting from a specific debtor company
- A letter writing service
- A forwarding service; many collection agencies have an affiliate network of attorneys who specialize in the filing of lawsuits to collect outstanding debts
- Reporting services; many collection agencies provide their customers with periodic progress reports on the status of their collection efforts

## Collection Agencies

Most commercial collection agencies in the U.S. operate on a contingent fee arrangement meaning that if nothing is collected they don't get paid. Contingent collection fees vary widely, even if and when their services and their collection results do not. It is important that the agency you select has these characteristics:

- It is professionally managed and experienced.
- It is accredited.
- The collection fee structure is competitive.
- The agency provides periodic written updates on its collection efforts.

Agreements should be put in writing covering these issues:

- How soon after the collection agency receives payment the creditor company will receive its money.
- That no settlement or payment plan will be made with a debtor without express, written approval from the creditor.
- That all communications and correspondence with the debtor will be handled in a professional and lawful manner.

## The Court System

The U.S. legal system is comprised of the Federal Court System which includes the U.S. Bankruptcy Courts as well as the court systems operated by each of the 50 states. Over 95% of the nation's legal cases are decided in state courts (or local courts acting as agents of the States). Generally, debt collection litigation is handled by state rather than federal courts. For an in-depth tutorial about the Federal Court System, please visit this website: http://www.uscourts.gov/FederalCourts.aspx

### Bankruptcy Laws

The more you know about the bankruptcy process, within reason, the more likely you will be able to reduce your risk. In the United States, the term "the Bankruptcy Code" generally refers to Title 11 of the United States Code, the federal bankruptcy law. Bankruptcy is a process governed primarily by federal law, and is used when people or companies cannot (or will not) pay their debts. Every company that extends open account credit to businesses will experience a customer bankruptcy sooner or later. As such, bad debt losses and bankruptcies are a cost of doing business on open account terms. To protect your company's interests, you must know the roles each these parties play in a bankruptcy:

- The bankrupt customer (the Debtor in Possession or DIP)
- The Bankruptcy Court
- The U.S. Trustee
- The Official Unsecured Credit Committee.

## Accounting Rules

In the United States, all publicly traded company's financial statements are required to be generated based on Generally Accepted Accounting Principles (GAAP) established by the Financial Accounting Standards Board (FASB). The FASB rules focus on improving the accuracy and usefulness of financial statements by focusing on the primary characteristics of relevance and reliability, and on the qualities of comparability and consistency. Publicly traded firms must use GAAP when presenting financial information to interested third parties in order to comply with U.S. securities laws.

## Usury Laws

Usury laws are established by each state in the United States. State laws place a legal maximum limit on the amount of interest that can be charged on consumer and commercial transactions. Usury involves charging an unconscionable or exorbitant rates of interest on a loan or debt. In other words, usury involves charging interest on a loan or debt higher than the law allows. In the United States, interest charged on certain types of debt is regulated by state law and cannot exceed the maximum rate provided by applicable state law. Information about usury laws by state can be found at: www.lectlaw.com/files/ban02.htm

## Escheatment Laws

To escheat unclaimed property means that the holder of that property delivers or transfers that property to the appropriate state governmental entity. Escheatment laws are commonly known as unclaimed property laws. Every State requires companies and financial institutions to report when property, cash or other assets have been abandoned or unclaimed by their owner and ultimately to deliver that property to the state when the owner cannot be found. The purpose of the law is to protect the rights of the owners of this property and their heirs as well as to provide a point of contact for the owners to recover their lost property in addition to providing a simple mechanism for making a claim for the return of unclaimed property.

## Statute of Limitations in Debt Collection

The Statute of Limitations is the period of time that a creditor or collector can use the courts to force a debtor to pay a debt. In fact, there are time limits associated with filing any type of lawsuit. Each state has laws defining the period during which a creditor may file a lawsuit to collect a delinquent balance from a debtor. Your attorney will be able to tell you the statute of limitations in the states in which your company does business. This link also provides information about state by state statutes of limitations: http://statelaws.findlaw.com/statutes-of-limitations.html

**Business Entities in the United States**

**Corporations:** A corporation is an entity created by state law capable of owning assets, incurring liabilities, and engaging in various business activities. A corporation is a legal entity separate from its shareholders, even if a single person happens to own all of the corporation's stock.

**Limited Liability Companies**: The owner - members of a limited liability company are protected from personal liability for the company's acts as well as for the acts of other members. Profits earned by a limited liability company are passed through to its members who pay personal income tax on those profits.

**Proprietorship:** A sole proprietorship is operated by one individual called the business owner. The owner's personal assets are at risk because they are considered to be intermingled with the assets and liabilities of the business.

**General Partnership:** A partnership is a voluntary association of two or more parties that exists to generate a profit. Each partnership is governed by a verbal or written agreement under the Uniform Partnership Act of 1996. Partners have unlimited personal liability for business debt.

### Software and technology

More and more American companies use dedicated credit management software to manage and optimize their order to cash process. From a technology point of view, there is a growing interest for big data (predictive analytics) and cloud solutions, including 24/7 inbound and outbound communication platforms but the latter is usually applied in B2C (business to consumer) environment. The focal points are: increasing efficiency and improving effective communication with customers. If you want to know more about the use and availability of credit management software and related applications in the United States, there is a great deal of information available online about credit risk management software, collection software, deduction management software, cash application software, and credit scoring software. One such website is: www.capterra.com/debt-collection-software .

## 1.2  Useful links about credit management, doing business and business culture in the USA

## Credit Management Services

### Bankruptcy

United States Courts: http://www.uscourts.gov/services-forms/bankruptcy

Nolo (for information about federal bankruptcy laws):

http://www.nolo.com/legal-encyclopedia/bankruptcy

### Country Risk Reports

Atradius is global credit insurer. An overview of country risk reports, can be found here: http://global.atradius.com/ccriskreport/list/ccriskreport.html

Coface is a global credit insurer sharing country risk information on its web-site: www.coface.com/Economic-Studies-and-Country-Risks

Euler Hermes is another global insurer who shares country ratings: www.eulerhermes.com/economic-research/Pages/Interactive-country-risk-map.aspx

Trading Economies is a useful resource, which provides country ratings by Moody's, S&P and Fitch: www.tradingeconomics.com/country-list/rating

 A global overview of country risk reports: www3.ambest.com/ratings/cr/crisk.aspx

### Credit information (B2B)

Cortera: www.cortera.com

Creditsafe: www.creditsafe.com

Dun&Bradstreet: www.dnb.com

For Credit Insurance companies (see below)

### Credit Insurance

www.icisa.org

ICISA is the International Credit Insurance Surety Association. Under "Publication" you can download the Yearbook 2014 2015, which provides a global overview of credit insurance companies in which countries they are active. The main credit insurance companies active in the United States are:

Atradius: www.atradius.us

Coface: www.cofacenorthamerica.com

Euler Hermes:www.eulerhermes.us

Zurich: www.zurichna.com

All of these companies offer a wide range of specialized products including debt collection services to enable companies to conduct business more safely both in the U.S. and overseas. One or more credit insurance companies may also specialize in specific business sectors.

## Credit Management Events

There is one main event for credit management in the United States.The Credit Congress and Expo". This attracts about 2,000 visitors a year and is usually held in May.

http://creditcongress.nacm.org

## Credit Management Information and services

Designed for business credit the Encyclopedia of Credit is a free resource specializing in topics related to corporate credit management. The Encyclopedia of Credit is sponsored by Credit Management Association.

www.encyclopediaofcredit.com

## Credit Management Software

Capterra provides information about top debt collection software products: http://www.capterra.com/debt-collection-software/

## Debt Collection & Debt Recovery

The **Atradius Debt Collection Handbook** (8th edition): www.atradiuscollections.com/global

The Atradius Debt Collection Handbook can be downloaded from this website. It contains information on debt collection procedures, rules and regulations in 40 countries, including the United States.

**Euler Hermes Economic research** "International debt collection – The Good, The Bad and the Ugly", in which debt collection in 44 countries is (briefly) analyzed including the United States.

www.eulerhermes.com/mediacenter/Lists/mediacenter-documents/Economic-Outlook-International-Debt-Collection-1213-dec14.pdf

## Legal system in the United States

http://global.practicallaw.com/country/united-states

Detailed information on the legal system in the United States, including bankruptcy, restructuring and insolvency.

www.lectlaw.com

The Lectric Law Library. An extensive source of information on the law system in the United States, including debt, debt collection, credit and bankruptcy.

# Doing business, business culture and credit management

Before you start doing business in the United States, it is always wise to contact your local United States consulate or the consulate of your country in the United States. Their advice is usually free of charge and they may be able to help you to get in touch with (local) business people who already have experience in doing business in the United States.

## Business culture and etiquette

Various websites about business culture, communication and business ethics in the United States:

www.executiveplanet.com/united_states-2/
http://guide.culturecrossing.net/basics_business_student.php?id=216
www.cyborlink.com/besite/us.htm
www.internations.org
www.worldguide.eu

## Credit Management & branch organizations

**NACM**: www.nacm.org : : American association of credit management companies

An advocate for business credit and financial management professionals, NACM is the primary learning, knowledge, networking and information resource for creditors.

NACM Affiliates: http://web.nacm.org/asp_aps/Affiliates/location/mmbr_map.asp

Credit and Financial Development Division: CFDD is focused on providing education, networking and professional support for employees of member firms of the NACM.

www.nacm.org/welcome-to-cfdd.html

**Credit Management Association**. One of the largest affiliates of the National Association of Credit Management (NACM). CMA delivers a variety of services to large and small companies across the full spectrum of the business credit economy.

http://creditmanagementassociation.org

**Commercial Law League of America**: www.clla.org
An organization that certifies debt collection companies that continue to meet the rigorous certification requirements of the CLLA.

**ICTF**. The association of International Credit and Trade Finance professionals

www.ictfworld.org

**FCIB**. International Association of Executives in Finance, Credit and International Business.

www.fcibglobal.com

## Doing business in the USA – country guides

Doing Business 2016 guide published by the World Bank. A complete source of information comparing business regulations for domestic firms in 189 economies.
www.doingbusiness.org

The Worldbank database: http://data.worldbank.org

## Factoring

RTS Financial: Provides an overview of factoring of accounts receivable:
http://www.rtsfinancial.com/guides/what-factoring

## LinkedIn Groups

- Credit Management Association (This is the largest NACM affiliate community on LinkedIn)
- Credit and Collection Management Professionals
- Credit Risk Group
- Credit and Collections
- Credit Risk Managers

Many U.S. based credit managers also join international credit and collections related LinkedIn groups.

## Payment behaviour

Credit insurance companies have a reasonably good insight into the payment behavior of companies in most economies. Companies including Atradius and Coface sometimes publish corporate payment survey results. Occasionally, D&B also publishes corporate payment studies.

Check your local credit information provider or credit insurance company for the latest data.

**Payment Practices Barometer Americas**, September 2015.
https://group.atradius.com/reports-and-advice/payment-practices-barometer-americas-2015.html

Check your local credit information provider or credit insurance company for the latest data.


## Payment systems and methods

A global database of (electronic) payment providers and payment methods.
www.about-payments.com/knowledge-base

## Public holidays & collection timing

It is a reasonable idea to make sure you get paid before national holidays. You can find the dates for national holidays (2015 and 2016) here: http://www.officeholidays.com/countries/usa/

# CHAPTER 2: COMMUNICATION WITH THE CUSTOMER

## 2.1 USA business culture and communication

Although most of the tips and suggestions from the previous chapter can be applied everywhere in the corporate world, you are likely to find subtle cultural differences in different countries. Ignoring these differences or not being aware of them can easily lead to misunderstandings, conflicts or disputes, which in credit management you want to avoid. In this paragraph, we will discuss the do's and don'ts in communicating with customers, in particular about late payment and related matters.

- Do remain calm. Focus on controlling your emotions and your behavior during collection calls
- Don't ignore disputes. Do try to address Issues before they become problems, and try to resolve problems before they become a crisis
- Do consider the possibility that you or your company may be wrong when a customer says there is a problem
- Do admit when you are wrong, and then take appropriate corrective action
- Don't hold grudges
- Do look for compromises. Consider brainstorming about possible solutions with the other person
- Do try to meet in person if there is a serious problem and phone calls and time are not resolving it

### American people in general

Citizens of the United States of America are known for being direct, open, friendly, pragmatic, creative and straightforward. At the same time and mainly because of their directness, Americans people may also be perceived as blunt or even rude. This direct approach can be easily misinterpreted by people from other cultures.

The American culture is a so-called low context culture, which means that many Americans like to communicate in a very explicit way. If you want a person to do something, you should best say it in a friendly but direct and clear way. In other words, don't make things unnecessarily complicated by being indirect.

However, directness has an advantage. It means that collectors can be direct. Americans can be open about a wide variety of topics, with the exception of personal or business finance. For example, it is not appropriate to ask someone about how much money they earn or their salary.

Even though Americans have a reputation of being friendly and open, many people are also quite fond of their privacy and can sometimes be rather conservative and reserved towards strangers. The degree of openness may vary significantly between younger and older generations as well as bigger cities and rural areas.

With regard to conservatism, you might be treated a bit cold or reserved if people don't know or trust you. Americans may consider themselves as culturally tolerant, but in reality they are not particularly tolerant. For foreigners, adapting to American business norms is key to success working with U.S. companies. Building relationships and establishing trust is important, both in personal as in business relationships. Another typical American characteristic is stubbornness. This characteristic does not apply to every American you meet, but some Americans have a sense of superiority. It might be argued that the best way to deal with this characteristic is simply to ignore it and move on to the next topic.

If you want a broader overview of American norms and American culture, consider reading: "93 Weird Things about the U.S. That Americans Don't Realize Are Weird" available at www.liberalamerica.org/2014/05/12/weird-things-about-americans/

### Rules and Regulations

Something very typical American is that many Americans dislike it when they "have to" do something. If you say to an American that she "has to do something" you can expect a response such as "*I don't have to do anything*" or "*Why should I have to do something? Because you say so!* So try to avoid the word "have to", but instead you may try to use a more indirect approach such as this: "*May I ask you to do this for me?*"

If you address an order as a question, the recipient is more willing to accept this. Another effective approach if people have to do something is to describe the goal first (for example prevent the account from being transferred to a collection agency) and indicate how to reach that goal (say to the customer that you need to receive payment before a specific date).

Here are some examples of statements or comments that should not be made to a delinquent debtor:

"*I'm only doing my job.*" In a sense, this is an apology. As the representative of a creditor calling to inquire about the status of a past due balance, you have nothing to apologize for. Why? Because your company is the damaged party, not the past due customer.

"*I'm sorry to bother you about this.*" This statement minimizes the importance of your collection call. You might want to substitute a statement such as this: "*Thank you for taking my call. I need your help to resolve a problem involving a balance of $xxx that has now become seriously delinquent.*"

"*If we cannot reach an agreement today relating to the past due balance, I am going to seriously consider placing your account for collection.*" A better way to state your expectation for the collection call and your intention to take action if the debtor cannot make a reasonable payment proposal would be to say: "*At the end of this discussion, if we have not negotiated some type of arrangement to retire the outstanding balance acceptable to your company and mine, I will be out of options and must immediately refer your account to a third party for collection.*"

*"I am under a lot of pressure to collect this past due balance as soon as possible. I could really use your help."* Any delinquent customer hearing this statement could be forgiven for assuming that they are in a strong bargaining position. Once the debtor is in the driver's seat or thinks she or he is in control, it is difficult for the collector to regain control of collection discussions and negotiate the fastest possible debt repayment.

*"I'm frustrated by the direction this discussion is taking."* This comment should not normally be used because (a) it is confrontational and (b) because its goal is to place the debtor on the defensive.

*"You must agree…"* A better option would be to indicate that you hope the customer will agree.

Also typically 'American' is the idea that there are rules and regulations for almost anything. One example is consumer debt collection: Consumer debt collection in the USA is highly regulated. In addition to state laws regulating debt collection, consumer debt collection is also subject to the federal regulations including but not limited to the provisions of the federal Equal Credit Opportunity Act as well as the Federal Fair Debt Collection Practices Act. The FDCPA is intended to protect consumers against overly aggressive or deceptive practices that might be used by an unscrupulous collector against an inexperienced and unsophisticated consumer, and collectors put their employers at risk if they do not understand or do not obey the laws governing consumer debt collection.

Everything in business needs to be organized and we need more rules to make sure that things stay organized. When working with customers, even if there are no laws addressing issues such as scheduling payment, there will almost certainly be internal processes and procedures you may need to circumvent in order to secure payment.

For example, you may consider to be obvious that if a customer has a $10,000 invoice and there is a $500 dispute that the customer would immediately pay the undisputed balance of $9,500. There are no laws that prevent them from doing so. However, the customer may have internal policies that prevent the accounts payable department from paying the undisputed balance. If and when this occurs, meaning when a customer offers an illogical reason for delaying payment, one of the most effective responses is for the collector to ask: *"Who do I need to speak with to secure a payment commitment today"*.

When dealing with public officials, try not to bend the rules or ask them to do so as you may achieve the opposite to the desired effect. In the United States, there are a number of state and federal laws and regulations intended to curtail any effort by government agents or officials to accept bribes or anything else of value to influence their decisions and actions. However, when rules start to limit their sense of freedom, which is considered a very important aspect of life, most American people will try to work around those rules, a slight but usually innocent form of anarchy.

## Humor

Collecting a past due balance is a serious matter. The use of humor, a humorous dunning notice, is unlikely to convince a chronically slow paying customer to pay more quickly and you risk not being taken seriously. Humorous messages in dunning notices and other collection correspondence are unusual in the United States. Proponents of the use of humorous labels, stickers, and stamps for use with monthly account statements and other dunning notices believe that a humorous request for payment is more likely to be noticed and acted upon. Humor should be used infrequently and sparingly.

## Complaining

For most Americans, complaining is part of everyday life and should not be taken too seriously. Complaining can also be seen as a way to share common joy or misery. People may complain about all kinds of things, but the weather and their children are two of the favorite topics and this is usually a good start to a conversation. It seems that actually the American weather is never good: it is too cold, too warm, too wet, too windy, but hardly ever good. It is part of the usual small talk at the beginning of a business conversation.

## Multicultural

You may also keep in mind that the American society is multicultural. Despite cultural tensions between American and some foreign cultures, generally speaking people are used to dealing with and living together with many different cultures, especially in the big cities. American people usually have a strong sense of equality. Discrimination based on skin color, age, sexual orientation, race or religion is unlawful. At the same time, foreigners living and working in the United States are expected to adjust their behavior to American norms, standards and customs.

## Yes and No

In America, in most cases 'Yes' literally means yes and 'No' literally means no. Saying No is not considered impolite if you respond to a specific direct question. This also fits into the straightforward, direct approach and mentality of many Americans. However, when you say "no" to a question, this may be countered by a "why" question. For example.

Collector: *"Can you pay the invoice before next Friday?"*

Customer: *"No, I cannot do that"*

Collector: *"Why? What is the reason why you cannot pay that past due invoice?"*

## Myths and Misconceptions

In the United States, there are any number of myths and misconceptions about the credit and collection function. It is important to be able to differentiate fact from fiction since collectors may base their actions on misconceptions and half-right assumptions, rather than facts.

Myth: It is both good manners and a good business practice to allow at least several days as a grace period before calling a customer to ask about the status of a past due balance.
Reality: Grace periods are unnecessary. There is nothing rude or inappropriate about asking a customer for payment status on any past due balance.

Myth: Credit departments often upset the apple cart by asking privately held companies for financial statements.
Reality: Request of this type are received routinely. The most common "reaction" to such a request is to ignore it.

Myth: Salespeople have nothing to contribute to the debt collection process.
Reality: Salespeople can sometimes bring additional pressure to bear to get a delinquent customer to open a dialogue with the credit department.

Myth: Export sales are often more trouble than they are worth.
Reality: Foreign sales can be lucrative opportunities for U.S. based companies trying to expand sales. However, export sales often present significantly higher risk than domestic sales, and it requires specialized skills and expertise to control this risk.

Myth: A company that is experiencing lower than expected bad debt losses is obviously doing a superior job of credit risk management.
Reality: There are no hard and fast rules about when bad debts must be recognized and written off. Even if actual losses are relatively low, the creditor company may be experiencing serious collection problems resulting in higher than forecasted DSO and causing the creditor company to experience cash flow problems that may in fact be serious enough to put the company at risk.

Myth: Credit professionals need to balance the needs of their organization with the need to maintain good business relationship with customers.
Reality: True, to some extent. However, the more flexibility you demonstrate when dealing with delinquent customers, the wider you open the door to abuse of your company's payment terms.


### Business & Private life

Business and private life are usually strictly separated. It occasionally happens that co-workers see each other after working hours or that friendships between colleagues grow. Personal friendships are rare even though people may work very well together and the relationship seems very friendly. Romantic relationships are also rare and are usually actively discouraged by employers. At work, one is supposed to act professionally and keep business and one's private life separate.

**Money and Showing off.**

Although the United States is a rich country, some people dislike it when others show off. If you wear expensive watches and clothing or drive an expensive car, some Americans may perceive you as a snob. Expensive things, when explicitly displayed, are not considered a sign of success --- with the possible exception of cars. If it appears to others that someone needs to surround herself or himself with material things to demonstrate to others that they are financially successful, such a person is commonly held in low esteem by some Americans. It is fine to be rich, but it is considered in poor taste to brag about it. This social norm helps explain America's love affair with cars and in particular with big, fast, loud, flashy cars that are often driven as a status symbol rather that based on their comfort or practicality.

**The Protestant Work Ethic**

A Protestant work ethic is a concept in sociology, economics, history and theology which emphasizes hard work, frugality and diligence as a constant display of a person's salvation, in contrast to the focus upon religious attendance, confession, and ceremonial sacraments of the Catholic faith.

In the American workforce, a person with Protestant work ethic internalizes the idea that inactivity is bad. Hard work is the source of self-esteem and therefore, as a working adult, sitting around in idleness brings immediate feelings of restlessness and guilt. The ideal day for an American worker who has internalized the Protestant work ethic is that a day when he/she manages to squeeze many tasks into the limited hours available is a good day. An often heard saying is: *"Never delay until tomorrow a task that could be completed today."*

Another often heard phrase is: *"Hard work is its own reward"*. Americans are comfortable what other people say you are good at your work, but you should never say it yourself. If you do, people will sooner or later challenge you and focus on your mistakes or revert to a personal Ad Hominem attack such as: *I don't care how good he is. He's a jerk, and the one thing I do know is that he is not as good as he thinks he is."*

So keep a low profile, be modest and work hard. If people ask about your work or experience, just say something like this: *"Well I have some experience in this field. I don't claim to be an expert but I have been doing this kind of work for more than fifteen years, so I know a few things about it."*

**Company culture, hierarchy, authority and decision making**

The company culture in American companies may of course vary from company to company. Generally speaking, it is rather informal meaning that people from different positions or roles can easily and directly communicate with each other. Though most American companies have a typical hierarchical structure, there is a low sense of hierarchy among American employees. Being the boss of a company means that you are responsible for the results of the company, but it does not automatically mean that people will accept or respect you. Authority, just like respect, needs to be earned.

American employees may voice their disagreement with their manager or senior management when they think he/she is making the wrong decision. Voicing concerns may even be appreciated if it offers constructive solutions that result in a better decision or outcome. Decision making can sometimes be a slow process because people may need to get approval for or agreement about certain decisions, however American workers are often given a significant amount of authority and autonomy to make decisions in the workplace.

### Ways of addressing people

Americans are much more straightforward in their approach to interpersonal communications than they were even ten years ago. Many American people don't mind if you address them by their first name, even if you have never met them before. When you speak to a person on the phone for the first time, each party will likely address the other on a first name basis. In most organizations, even executive management including the CEO or CFO are called by their first names by employees at every level in the company. However, you might give some consideration to being more tactful with older people or people in higher positions if you don't know them very well.

### Regional differences

In America, there can be subtle differences regional differences in business norms. Below you will find a very brief overview of the regional differences in the U.S.A. Keep in mind that this a generalization and that there are always exceptions to the rule.

**Western U.S.** Business in California is usually informal. Employees including executives tend to dress down for work. Decision making authority is highly distributed.

**Middle America.** People are more formal than in the West. People usually prefer less familiarity in business settings. People living in Middle America consider themselves to be work hard and representing the center and the backbone of America. You will find a lot of industry this part of the country.

**The South.** Well known cities include Atlanta, and Dallas. People who live in the South are considered conservative. A well-known expression is that someone in the South is *"Below the Mason-Dixon line"*, which geographically indicates the border between North and the South. The South is sometimes called the Bible belt, referring to the importance of Christianity and in particular fundamentalist Christianity. American people from the South usually prefer some small talk before you start to talk about business. Jokes are also appreciated, but only when you have known each other for a longer period of time.

**East.** In this part of the United States, you will find cities like New York. People from this part of the country are straightforward and some might say blunt. In general, people from this area are considered to be hard working and straightforward. To some, this direct manner of communication and the candor of verbal and written communication may appear aggressive or even confrontational.

### Politics and religion

In many countries, people do not discuss sex, politics or religion in a business setting. This is not necessarily the case in the United States. There are many Americans who will eventually get around to discuss one of these topics. However, it is best to avoid those topics in business conversations, as it can easily lead to conflicts and escalations. Try to keep your conversation to business and small talk, but stay away from sex, politics and religion.

### Effective Communication in credit management

The direct and open approach of the American is often also reflected in the way American credit management is practiced. People in credit management are usually quite practical and straightforward in their communication, though that may also depend on the business culture within a company. Collectors often have cash collection targets, which can sometimes lead to conflict with the sales department.

Every company will have its own style or preference in communication with customers, but the telephone is the most commonly used tool and is considered by most collectors to be the best and most effective and most efficient collection mechanism. Here is the rationale: A dunning letter or friendly reminder notice is a form of one-way communication and as such can be easily ignored. Calling customers is a very common business practice and usually very effective, provided you approach the customer in a non-aggressive and customer-friendly way. Be direct, make some small talk or go straight to the topic. The good thing about personal contact is that you can use that moment to also work on the relationship with the customer.

### Calling or sending reminder letters.

Calling customers about outstanding overdue invoices and if necessary confirming in writing afterwards is more effective than just sending reminders or dunning letters. A call may start with some small talk, depending on the kind of person. Then it usually goes straight down to the topic. The way you address the topic may vary from person to person. Just like in sales, a credit controller should try to communicate in line with how he thinks is the best or most effective tone of voice to create an atmosphere where the customer is willing to communicate and work towards a solution (payment, promise to pay, question, resolution, etc.).

Here are some basic collection tips for doing business in the United States:

- Always remain polite and professional.
- Start your collection discussion by asking for immediate payment of the entire past due balance.
- Never make a concessions until you have received enough information to conclude that the customer needs and deserves additional time to pay the past due balance.
- Set specific and measurable goals for collection calls.

- Try not to leave voice mail messages. If you must leave a message, give your name and telephone number at the beginning and the end of the message. Always ask for a return telephone call the same day.
- If there is an order on hold as a result of the delinquent status of the account, make sure that this information is communicated to accounts payable.
- Don't use your speaker-phone. It is considered rude.
- Don't rush, and don't allow the debtor to rush through the discussion.
- Keep personalities out of the collection discussion. Always avoid confrontations.
- Avoid arguments. Seek solutions.
- Follow up promptly on any broken payment commitment. Ask: "*Why did it happen?*" "*Why you were not notified, and when the payment will be made?*"
- Make certain your collection calls are interactive. If the customer is not communicative, be direct. Ask for their comments and feedback.
- Challenge the decision-maker to provide a better commitment if the commitment made is something other than immediate payment in full.
- If a customer has a history of making and then breaking commitments, confirm their commitment in writing. Better yet, arrange for them to confirm their commitment to you in writing.
- Take careful notes and be sure you know the full name and title of the person you are speaking to or negotiating with about payment.

In general, business relationships are considered important, but it is also important is to get paid on time. Many American companies are pragmatic in their approach, where a deal is deal and it is generally expected that you keep your promises. As such, credit management can actually be seen as financial relationship management. When dealing with the American a direct, respectful and customer friendly approach is usually effective.

# 12 excuses for late payment and how to deal with them

Below we have listed 12 excuses. We will discuss each excuse in detail, provide an example and show you how to deal effectively with each excuse.

1. *We never received the invoice*
2. *We always pay our invoices after 60 days*
3. *I just paid the invoice*
4. *I really don't understand it. I paid a few days ago*
5. *The payment has not been authorized, because the person responsible for approving invoices (departmental manager or general manager) is not available/out of the office.*
6. *We never received the goods*
7. *My customer has not paid me yet*
8. *The invoice was incorrect and I am still waiting for a credit note*
9. *The order was cancelled*
10. *My customer went bankrupt.*
11. *The financial paperwork is at my accountant's office.*
12. *The managing director is on vacation and he needs to approve the payment.*

## EXCUSE #1

**Customer:** '*We never received the invoice.*'

**Supplier**: '*If I send you a copy by email today, can you arrange to pay us before Friday?* [If there is a reason to doubt the customer's statement, you can indirectly indicate that not receiving an invoice is a very rare event, so the customer will have to think of another excuse in the future]

### Explanation

This excuse is frequently used and may be true. Although delivery times may vary from country to country and guarantees of delivery are not provided, most invoices you mail ultimately arrives at its destination. If it is a particularly high value or important invoice, you may want check your local postal service for estimated delivery times, traceability and possibly use an overnight delivery service such as DHL or UPS.

A customer who claims that he did not receive the invoice, often, but not always, means that the customer has lost the invoice or incorrectly 'filed' the invoice (i.e. the invoice lies somewhere in the proverbial pile of documents to be processed. In other words, the administration is probably a mess). If you notice that the same customer frequently uses this excuse, it is a good idea to monitor the customer more closely. For future deliveries, you could contact the customer a few days after the delivery took place to make sure the customer has received the invoice. If the customer wants to know the reason for your call, you can tell respond that it is important to you that invoices are produced promptly and arrive addressed to the correct person. After all, it is important for both the customer and the supplier that invoices are correct and sent and delivered in a timely manner. By dealing with the situation in this way, you will leave a professional impression, improve customer experience and, over time, it may lead to improved payment behavior by your customer.

## EXCUSE #2

**Customer:** *'We always pay our invoices after 60 days.'*

**Supplier:** *'I hear what you are saying, but, our terms and conditions clearly state that your payment terms are net 30 days and you know that. I would like to talk to you about how we can prevent these payment issues in the future?'* Alternative: *'I hear what you are saying, but how would you feel if I bought goods from you on net 30 days, but then paid after 60 days?'* [wait for their response and then dig deeper into the topic]

## Explanation

Customers can sometimes be very creative by inventing their own payment terms. The explanation for such behavior is not always clear, but often these types of customers think that they are so important to a supplier that they will be happy to do business with them no matter what payment terms they might invent. In such cases, it can be very difficult to get the customer back in line. On the one hand, it would not be fair to allow one or a few customers to have different, more favorable terms.  On the other hand, you may not want to offend the customer and possibly lose their business. It takes patience and a clear strategy, to know what to do with such customers. Therefore you need to understand the future commercial importance of such customers and discuss with the sales department how to proceed. Changing payment behavior is often a time consuming process. Being consistent and reminding the customer of the terms in a friendly way will maintain the relationship and may improve payment behavior. However, if this doesn't work you need to decide, in conjunction with the sales department, whether to continue the customer relationship or gradually say goodbye.

## EXCUSE #3

**Customer:** *'I just paid the invoice'*

**Jenkins:** *'That's good news. Did you pay the invoice electronically?'* [wait for a reply] *'When did you pay the invoice (or outstanding amount)?'* [wait for a reply]. Alternative: *'How much did you pay and where was the payment sent?'* [wait for a reply]? *'If you paid yesterday, it should be visible on our statement tomorrow at the latest. I will check then.  Thanks for your time.'*

## Explanation

This reply is probably the one you will hear the most and it is very easy for the customer to use. However, you can easily check if the customer is telling you the truth or not. An electronic payment processed by the customer cannot be reversed, unless the bank refuses to execute the transaction due to lack of funds or insufficient credit. During the conversation, you don't need to tell the customer you will contact him again if you do not receive the payment within one or two days. You will contact the customer anyway if the payment doesn't show up on your bank statement. When a customer uses this excuse, often it may indicate that you are dealing with an undisciplined or unorganized customer. It may also mean that they are in a poor financial position, so when in doubt you better check their creditworthiness. With these types of customers, it is important to stay in close control and send reminders shortly after the due date. A proactive, but customer-friendly, reminder strategy may work as well. Credit management software and automated collections strategies can obviously help a lot to improve payment behavior.

## HINT

If you ask the customer to send a copy or print screen of the electronic payment, be aware that the payment has actually been processed, so the customer cannot delete the payment instruction afterwards. However, a payment that has been instructed does not necessarily mean that the payment is processed. If the credit limit or overdraft facility of your customer with his bank has been exceeded, the bank may decide not to execute the payment instruction. One of the fastest and most reliable ways of getting paid is by phone payment (telephone banking), where your bank confirms receipt of the payment via email or by telephone.

## EXCUSE #4

**Customer:** *'I really don't understand it. I paid that a few days ago.'*

Jenkins: *'A couple of days ago I talked to you and you told me that you paid the outstanding invoice/invoices. What has happened, did the bank not process your payment?'* [wait for a reply] *'Well, if you could arrange a payment today we can clear the account.'* [optional] *'Could you call me when you have processed the payment and I can check our account to confirm receipt of the payment? Is that OK with you?'* [wait for a reply] *'Great, I look forward to receiving the payment. I hope you have a good day and I am pleased we could resolve this issue.'*

## Explanation

If you have to call the customer because they did not meet their commitment to pay you on a specific date, it usually means one of two things:

1) The customer simply did not make the payment

2) The bank has not approved the payment instruction due to a negative balance or other financial problems with the customer's account.

The first case suggests that you are dealing with a lazy or unreliable customer. The second case may mean that your customer has liquidity or cash flow problems, so you also need to check the creditworthiness of the customer. If your customer faces financial troubles, it is unlikely to tell suppliers about it. At the same time, it can be a huge relief for the customer to know that supplier is willing to listen and think about ways to help resolve the problem.

Especially when financial problems are temporary, it can help both the customer and the supplier to openly discuss the matter, ideally you can both find practical and realistic solutions. Also, don't forget to inform the sales department, so that they know what going on with their account.  In both cases, it is important to monitor the customer closely over the next few months and find a way to improve their payment behavior.

## EXCUSE #5

**Customer:** '*The payment has not been authorized, because the person responsible for approving invoices (departmental manager, procurement manager or general manager) is not available/out of the office.*'

Jenkins: '*I thought that you were responsible for all payment processes? Who needs to authorize this invoice and when will they be back?*' [wait for a reply] '*Does this mean that future payments will be delayed?*' [wait for a reply] '*Obviously, I am not very pleased about this. The invoices are already way past due, so we need (stronger: have to) to find a solution today. Can you contact the person who can authorize payments? I will call you at [time] to see where we go from here. Is that OK?*' [wait for a reply]

## Explanation

Hiding behind decision makers or procedures is something you will find in all kinds of organizations, especially within larger ones. Just when you need person X, he is not there or in a meeting. Large companies often work with so called payment procedures as a part of the procurement process. The invoice may be authorized, but when payment isn't, you still won't get your money. In practice it is very tough, if not impossible, to bypass these procedures. The best thing you can do is to build a good relationship with your contact in the accounts payable department. It will probably not change the authorization procedure, but you may get a higher payment priority on the list of suppliers. It depends on the commercial and strategic importance of the customer as to what measures and adjustments of collections strategies you need to consider when this problem occurs often.

## HINT /TIP 1

Sometimes, it can be hard to reach someone by phone to talk about outstanding invoices. In these situations, it may help to let a colleague from sales or account management call the customer and ask for the same person. Customers with liquidity problems often don't like to talk about it. However, business does go on, so when your customers depend on deliveries for their own business to continue, they will still want to talk to people from sales. Once your sales or account manager has your contact on the line, he can easily put them through to the credit department. Therefore a good relationship between sales and credit management is essential, so you can team up if required.

## HINT /TIP 2

If you suspect that you are being ignored because your contact is hard to get on the phone, then you may have to try alternative methods. Maybe the admin is blocking you from talking to the decision maker. In this situation, it is important to stay in close control and get the secretary 'involved' in your goal. A very simple but effective method is asking direct questions, such as: 'When did you see or talk to Mr. X' or 'Did you pass on my message to Mr. X.? What did he say?' or 'Why did Mr. X. not call me?' By asking these types of questions it will become more difficult for the admin to maintain her role of protecting her boss. Remember to stay friendly and asking the right questions can be a very effective way to get to where you want to be; in this scenario you want to talk to the managing director.

**ATTENTION!** Regarding payment issues, liquidity or cash flow problems, be aware that you **do not** discuss these with anyone other than your accounts payable contact at the customer. Payment problems can sometimes be very sensitive and the customer will probably not appreciate it if you discuss the company's financial problems with a random employee. So always be discrete when you talk about late payments or overdue invoices.

## EXCUSE #6

**Customer:** *'We never received the goods!'*

Jenkins: *'I will immediately check with our shipping department, one moment please.'* [call the shipping manager and ask if they can confirm the delivery and can send a copy of a signed proof of delivery]. *'If you didn't receive the goods, did your receive the invoice?'* [If the answer is yes.] *'Why didn't you contact us earlier, since I assume that you ordered and need the goods we delivered that you ordered?'* [wait for a reply] (meanwhile you have received a copy of the signed delivery note from the dispatch department). *'I just received a signed copy of the delivery receipt which indicates that you have received and signed for the goods. I will email a copy of the proof of delivery to you now, so you can have a look at it and check on it. I will give you a call in an hour, so we can discuss payment of the outstanding amount?'* [wait for a reply]

## Explanation

Every new customer should receive a copy of your terms and conditions. In these terms and conditions, there is (or should be) y a section about non-delivery or disputes and how the customer should deal with them. This should include a time period in which claims for non-delivery or short delivery should be addressed with the supplier. So a customer claiming that they have not received the goods but did receive the invoice, is actually violating the terms and conditions. It may also indicate poor administration and handling of incoming goods by your customer. If this excuse is used often by the same customer, then it is advisable to monitor the customer more closely with regard to confirmation of receipt of goods.

It may be worth asking your shipping department to call the customer after the next few deliveries to confirm that the correct quantity and type of goods have been received.

## HINT

When the goods arrive at the customer a delivery note needs to be signed, but also make sure that the name of the recipient is clearly readable (preferably get them to print their name underneath the signature). In practice and in particular when the driver is in a hurry the (electronic) delivery note often only has a (digital) signature but does not mention a name. When a delivery is disputed, it can save a lot of time if the name of the recipient is clear. Instruct your drivers or give clear instructions to your external logistics partner.

## EXCUSE #7

**Customer:** *'My customer has not paid me yet.'*

Jenkins: *'I am sorry to hear that, but does that mean that you can't pay any invoices anymore?'* [wait for a reply]? *'Of course it is frustrating that your customer hasn't paid you, but I am afraid that this is not an excuse not to pay us. Can you make a payment today?'* [wait for a reply] *'When do you expect your customer to pay you?'* [wait for a reply]. [Alternative 1]: *'We have to pay our suppliers and employees on time, so it is important that our customers (including you) pay us on time.'* [Alternative 2, if nothing else works] *'OK, as soon as you receive payment from your customer, which you are expecting on* [date expected payment], *can we agree that you will immediately pay the outstanding invoice(s).'* [wait for confirmation].

## Explanation

This excuse is not only a poor one, but from a customer's point of view it is not a very smart one either. Often this excuse is an indication that your customer is experiencing liquidity or cash flow problems. It may also say something about the customer's credit management policy. However, if you have a good relationship with your customer you should be able to discuss the issue openly and work on a practical solution. If progress is a bit sluggish, you could always try to turn the situation around and ask the customer how he would feel or act if he was in your position (tip 24). By confronting the customer with his own excuse, they will see that this excuse is irrelevant and harms more than it helps the customer's position.

When the customer tells you they expect their customer to pay soon and then they will be able to pay you. If the account is not seriously overdue, you may accept this. Accepting this kind of excuse should be an exception, so you don't give your customer the idea they can get away with it every time, by establishing a precedent. When this kind of excuse is used frequently by the same customer, always check the creditworthiness of the customer and discuss this with sales.

## EXCUSE #8

**Customer:** *'The invoice was incorrect and I am still waiting for a credit memo.'*

Jenkins: *'What exactly is wrong with the invoice?'* [wait for a reply] In this case, it seems that the wrong discount was applied: 5% when it should have been 15%. *'When did you realize this mistake?'* [wait for a reply] or *'Why didn't you let us know earlier, because now the invoice is now overdue?'* [wait for a reply] *'Surely you checked the invoice on receipt? It is common practice to notify us of any problems with invoices within five working days. In future you, will you let us know as soon as possible? I will make sure that you receive a credit memo or a corrected invoice as soon as possible. I will also flag our system so that this problem does not happen again. I will let you know when the credit memo is issued. In the interim, you can arrange for an immediate payment of the balance that is not in dispute? Does that work for you?'* [wait for a reply]

## Explanation

Questions and inquiries regarding incorrect invoices, deliveries or damaged goods should always take place within the timescale as stated in your terms and conditions. Since such inquiries regarding incorrect invoices, prices or discounts, are frequently made after the invoice is due for payment, it is important to pay extra attention to this category. In contrast, in the case of incorrect deliveries, your customer will most likely call you the same day. Of course it can sometimes happen that the customer forgets to let you know. Always check if claims for incorrect deliveries are valid or not and conduct analysis afterwards. Ultimately, the errors that result in disputes and claims should be kept to a minimum by the seller because they have a negative impact on the business process, costs, cash flow and the customer relationship. If issues are frequently raised only after the invoice is due, it is a good idea to temporarily check with the customer about new deliveries and invoices soon after goods are delivered and the customer is invoiced. Also, discuss underlying problems resulting in disputes with the relevant departments such as operations, shipping, sales and order entry.

## EXCUSE #9

**Customer:** *'The order was cancelled.'*

Jenkins: *'I can't see any notification on our system. Who did you discuss this with and when?'* [wait for a reply]. *'Did you cancel the order by telephone or in writing?'* [wait for a reply]. [When the customer informs you long after the delivery was made] *'Why didn't you call us as soon as you received the goods?'*[wait for a reply]. *'One moment please, I will contact our sales department.'* [following the conversation]. *'I just spoke with our sales department and they haven't received any cancellation notice for that order. Before I make a decision, I would like to discuss it with your salesperson or account manager and then call you back to finalize the matter. Is that ok with you?'*

After talking to the salesperson, it appears that he knows nothing about the cancellation. In fact, the order was placed at the customer's office and signed by him. The salesperson decides that this order should not be taken back. You call the customer back.

'*I have talked to* [name of salesperson], *and he confirmed that you placed and signed the order at your office. This means that the order and delivery is valid and that the invoice should be paid.*' [wait for a reply]. In this case, the customer accepts the position. '*Now that we have resolved the problem would you arrange payment of the outstanding invoice this week?*'

## Explanation

It happens to all of us that we sometimes make a mistake or that the market suddenly changes and as a result we want to cancel an order. It can also happen that a supplier sometimes ships an order that was previously cancelled by the customer. No matter what the reason, the customer needs to communicate with the seller about incorrectly delivered orders or the delivery of cancelled orders in a timely manner. A good customer relationship can be very helpful, but prerequisites are transparency, honesty and timely communication from both sides. If the customer just responds when the supplier calls regarding an overdue invoice, then you could say the customer has acted negligently. The standard rule is that issues with any shipped order not identified within a couple of days of delivery, should be considered a normal fulfilled order that has to be paid for within the usual terms.

On the other hand, don't play hard ball unnecessarily when the customer has accidentally made a mistake. Especially in cases in which cancellation of an order is a rare event, don't make too much fuss about it and simply give in to the customer's wishes. Being flexible and bearing the costs of picking up the goods often benefits the customer relationship and future sales. Always make sure that your customers know how to act when they want to cancel an order and also instruct your sales people, so they can inform the customer as well.

Also make sure that your business processes and procedures are robust and easy to understand, so you will avoid unnecessary mistakes. This is usually a joint effort between sales, logistics, finance, credit management, service and IT. By efficiently working together, you can save a lot of time and costs, which benefits both the supplier and the customer.

## EXCUSE #10

**Customer**: '*My customer went bankrupt.*'

Jenkins: '*I am sorry to hear that. What does this mean for your organization?*' [wait for a reply] '*How did this happen? Were you taken by surprise?*' [the answer will give you more of an insight into the quality of your customer's credit (risk) management] '*I understand it must be very inconvenient and difficult for you, but if you went bankrupt tomorrow, should I tell my suppliers that I can't pay them for the time being?*' [wait for a reply] '*Despite your current cash flow problems, it is important that we find a solution. When do you expect to be able to pay us?*' [wait for a reply] '*Two months? That seems a bit of a long time to me. I would suggest a payment plan/schedule under which you will pay* [amount part payment] *for the next (number of) weeks.*' [optional] '*Until you have fully paid the outstanding amount, we are happy to ship new orders on a cash in advance basis.*'

## Explanation

If a client of your customer goes bankrupt this could have a temporary negative impact on your customer's liquidity. Although a bankruptcy cannot always be predicted, it may say something about the quality and consistency of your customer's credit management process and the way they monitor the creditworthiness of their customers. If a bankruptcy seriously impacts your customers liquidity or capacity to pay, this is an indication that your customer's financial status and liquidity is not very strong and you need to be more alert with this customer or issue a new credit check. Of course, a bankruptcy is an unpleasant and sometimes costly experience, but with proper credit (risk) management in place you should not experience this too often and it should not significantly impact a company's capacity to pay. A customer who tells you that due to the bankruptcy of one of his customers he cannot pay you, actually reveals more about his financial status and creditworthiness than he may realize.

## EXCUSE #11

**Customer**: '*The financial paperwork is at my accountant's office.*'

Jenkins: '*When will your accountant return the paperwork?*' [wait for a reply] '*In two weeks? Can I suggest that since the invoices are well overdue, I send you a copy of them by email, so you can arrange payment today? Is that alright with you?*' [wait for a reply]

## Explanation

This excuse can't be used by the customer too often. After all, how many times a year do you visit your bookkeeper or accountant and leave all your paperwork? Using this excuse implies that your customer would also not be able to pay other suppliers, which is quite unlikely. When used more frequently, it is often an indication of financial problems. The best way to deal with this excuse is to send the customer a copy of the invoice(s) and ask they be paid immediately. If the customer still refuses to cooperate, you can always tell the customer that slow payment may delay new deliveries or in the worst case put the customer on stop.

## EXCUSE #12

**Customer:** '*The CFO is on holiday and he needs to approve the payment.*'

Jenkins: '*When will your CFO return?*' [wait for a reply] '*And does this mean that you can't pay other suppliers as well?*' [wait for a reply] '*Unfortunately, since the outstanding invoices are seriously overdue, if you cannot arrange payment all shipments may be delayed.*' [this is a friendly way of saying that the customer is put on delivery hold/stop]. '*How can we resolve this problem?*'[wait for a reply]? If the customer doesn't want to cooperate, you can apply more pressure. '*I really don't want to put you on stop, but you leave me no choice unless you pay the overdue invoices. I hope you understand my position. If you can pay earlier, please give me a call. Otherwise I would suggest you make an urgent payment as soon as your CFO has returned from his holiday.*' [wait for a reply] '*OK I will contact you on* [the date the CFO returns], *so we can resolve the matter.*'

## Explanation

A CFO who 'suddenly' goes on holiday and doesn't leave clear instructions for his staff, or doesn't authorize one or two employees to make payments is, in fact, an example of poor management. It is not only bad to act like this, but it also leaves a bad impression about the mentality of their supplier (relationship) management. It is also bad for the employees, because they are not able to resolve financial matters if required. This is clearly not the way to do business and a chat with the CFO when he returns from holiday wouldn't hurt. In a good and productive customer relationship, it should be possible to say that you are not pleased with this kind of behavior. Prevention is always best, so pay a bit more attention to your customers before the holiday season starts and make clear arrangements with your customers about payments during the holidays so you can avoid the situation described above.

### Dealing with late payment excuses.

The schedule below may be helpful in showing how you can deal with excuses for late payment. With a lot of practice and listening to your customers and colleagues, you will automatically learn how to deal with almost any excuse in an effective and customer-friendly way.

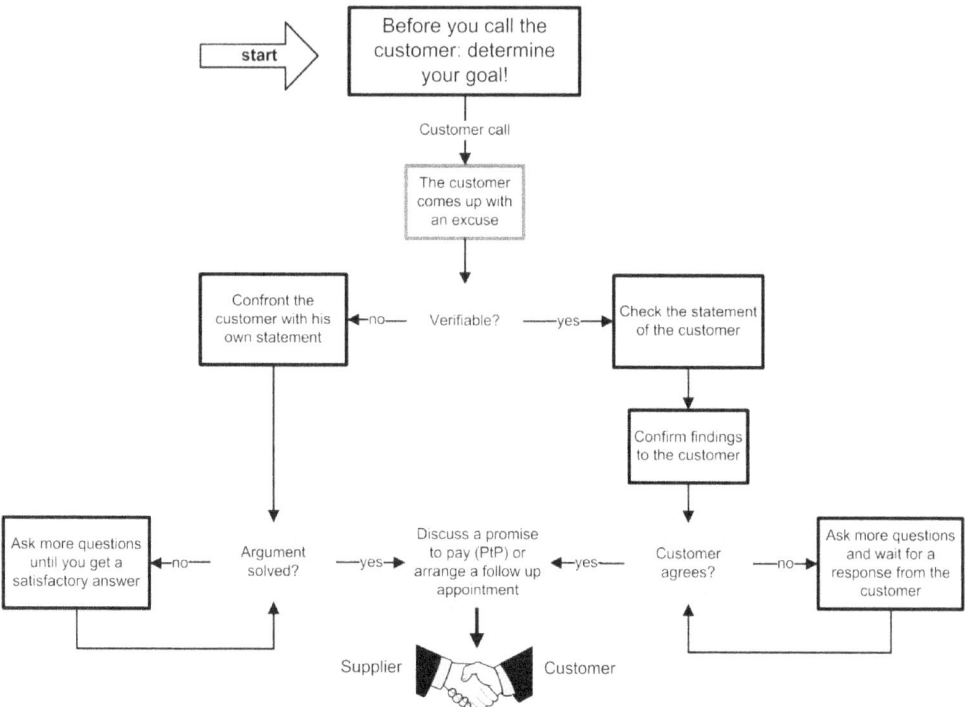

**Figure 1: Flowchart dealing with excuses**

# The authors

## Michael C. Dennis

Michael C. Dennis is a partner in CoveringCredit.com, a credit and collection consulting company located in California. Michael is the author or co-author of four books including: "The Credit and Collection Handbook" and "Credit and Collection Forms and Procedures Manual." He has been a featured speaker at numerous national and regional credit conferences. Michael works as a part-time instructor for the Credit Management Association as well as for the Wisconsin Credit Association. Michael has also taught the CAP and ACAP programs intended for working credit and collection professionals for more than ten years. Michael received an M.B.A. from Pepperdine University, and received the Credit Business Fellow Accreditation from the National Association of Credit Management.

www.coveringcredit.com

## Marcel Wiedenbrugge

Marcel Wiedenbrugge is managing director of WCMConsult. Marcel combines knowledge and experience in account management/sales, credit management, service management and related software solutions. In the past he worked for companies like Ricoh, Van Ommeren Ceteco, PCD Polymere and Yamaha Musical Instruments Europe.
Most of the time he worked in a B2B environment, but he is also quite familiar with retail. Marcel is an entrepreneur, speaker, writer, researcher, trainer and consultant. He develops, organizes and conducts workshops, trainings and seminars. He frequently writes articles and is the author of several books.

www.wcmconsult.com                    marcel.wiedenbrugge@wcmconsult.com

## Cliff Wynn

Cliff Wynn is managing director of RK Business Training Ltd. Cliff has both experience of working in the training, collections and tracing industry for many years. He has also worked with and for many of the leading professional bodies within the credit and collections industry, including the role of Head of Training for the Institute of Credit Management. He has built up a considerable knowledge of running a training business plus has 'hands on' experience of telephone and doorstep collections, compliance, consumer credit licence applications and tracing. During his career Cliff has worked with many large organisations on various training programmes in the collections area. Clients have included, Orange, Shell, Marston Group, Brighthouse, NPower, British Gas, Polycom BV, and the Finance and Leasing Association.

www.rkbusinesstraining.co.uk                    cliff@rkbusinesstraining.co.uk

## Notes

# Notes